Carol —
Thanks fo
your help
everything else.

Dan Sul

The Ancient Art of B.S.

Essay One

By Dan Sullivan

B.S.
Essay One

Table of Contents

Introduction...4

I. Prelude 8

II. What is Bullshit? 14

III. The Cogito.......................................28

Appendix I: The Origins of Bullshit 36

Introduction

Please be aware that, for the sake of clarity—and, as well, my own sense of elegance in the written word—I will, for the remainder of this essay, which is the first of a series on the subject, dispense with the abbreviation B.S. in favor of the vulgar honesty of the word that stands behind it: *bullshit.*

That is correct. This is the beginning of an essay series about bullshit, about bullshitting, about spinning a web of lies, half-truths, fantasies, and personas around the actual, grim truth of an aspect or aspects of our lives. It is also about the *bullshit artist.*

It is my hope that all who read this series, these pamphlets of impurity in discourse (which, in substance, are themselves *bullshit* of a sort) will emerge from the reading as themselves *master bullshit artists.*

Which is to say this essay series is intended to be both a description of bullshit and an instruction regarding *how* to bullshit well (and *why* to do so, as well as *when*). There is beneath the veneer of tongue-in-cheek tone in this series a serious and all-pervasive truth: life without bullshit is not a life worth living. Life without bullshit would be strikingly bland and remarkably without colorful scent. So sniff in the rich aroma of the bullshit that surrounds you—and appreciate it with me as we move onward into the cesspool!

Let us then explore this seemingly grotesque subject. Let's dig into it. Let's get our hands dirty, as well as our minds. Forward then. Get ready. Keep your pants on ... or, well—don't.

You might consider reading this series of essays while seated on the toilet.

That would be a most suitable reading perch for a treatise on bullshit.

I guarantee that each essay should be good for at least one, maybe two visits to the water closet, depending of course upon your constitution.

Above all, I hope your life is enriched by my exploration of this most worthy subject.

Daniel Sullivan
Chicago, IL
2018

I. Prelude

"To thine ownself be true."
— Polonius (Hamlet)

There are those who would criticize bullshit as disingenuous. We have an image of the bullshit artist: a puffed up blithering idiot pretending he knows what he is talking about when, in fact, he knows little to nothing. Sometimes he takes the form of a teacher, or a boss, or even the President of the United States. You see him and you are disgusted that such a know-nothing could have achieved the authority to speak on a subject of which he is almost entirely ignorant. But he does it. Oh, does he do it! The words flow trippingly from his tongue. He is utterly confident even as his speech on the subject moves further and further into what you think is pure error. But by the end of the master bullshit artist's speech, you yourself are astonishingly beginning to question your own suppositions on the subject. Maybe the bullshit artist could be

right about some of what he said ...
maybe, just maybe ...

One of the greatest examples of a
master bullshit artist is Polonius from
Shakespeare's *Hamlet*. At least, that's my
opinion. Some may differ. But let's focus
on my take on things, since I am writing
this treatise on bullshit.

Why poor Polonius? In Act I Scene 3
of *Hamlet,* as Polonius prepares to send
his young Laertes into the world, the old
man provides Laertes with advice that is,
in my estimation, pure bullshit. It is
conflicted, haphazard. It is advice
manufactured quickly to sound like good

advice by a man who thinks he should give advice in this situation but does not know how.

"Give thy thoughts no tongue," begins Polonius, advising Laertes not to speak his mind. Polonius then follows with a series of directives to Laertes on various disconnected scenarios, such as how to deal with quarrels and recommendations on avoiding borrowing or lending money.

But, in the end, Polonius makes a statement that echoes even now through the history of literature and the literature of history (even though very few know that this line is the tail end of an elderly man's bullshit ramble in *Hamlet.*). That statement: *"Above all, to thine ownself be true."*

As you can then see, the bullshit artist, in his relentless, dedicated pursuit to provide advice of value, even when he seems to have no advice of value to give, produces a nugget, a golden kernel of truth that speaks not just to the fictional Laertes, but to legions of real men and women. Written on many chips given to Alcoholics Anonymous members for achieving periods of sobriety are these words: *To Thine Ownself Be True.* Might I posit then that the master bullshit artist is a creator of wisdom—wisdom he or she might not at the onset possess, but which emerges as part of the process of bullshitting.

Still, bullshit can most certainly be annoying. I will admit that, of course. It is painful to listen to much of the bullshit which besieges us in day-to-day life.

II. What is Bullshit?

"Bullshit is the glue that binds us as a nation."
— George Carlin

The proliferation of bullshit in our post-modern or post-post-modern world is rampant, encouraged, and necessary. As George Carlin said, it is the very "glue" which binds our nation—all nations, really—together. That is because bullshit is, in fact, a kind of fabric of reality spun together by the bullshit artists of any era.

It is the stuff from which the dream of civilization is born. We are all part and parcel of bullshit.

But what is this bullshit so integral to the maintenance of our civilization? It involves, through spoken or written word, the creation of ideas about ourselves that raise us up above the status of being mired in grim fact. For fact, if left to itself, drags us down into an unforgiving cesspool. The reality of life is that for all of us, no matter our stature, it ends up six feet under. In the meantime, during that brief flicker of life between birth and death, we are compelled to spin stories of meaning that transform the reality that levels us all. Perhaps it is human nature to spin stories, something we inherited in the evolutionary survival of the fittest, that, perhaps ironically, those most fit to survive are those who can transform the factual into the artificial, who can transcend the survival of the fittest, and survive, even by denying its existence and committing to stories of creationism that do not conform with our current science of life.

But what is our current science of life but bullshit of another caliber? Darwin's theories, though supported by some evidence, remain, as of yet, unproven. That said, the theory of evolution itself is a beautiful and elaborate piece of bullshit, born of the culture of its day and fostered by our own culture, meant to bring sense to facts that are beyond sense—i.e., the fact of existence itself. That we have no conception of how life began, why it began, or why and how it ends—these inspire us to invest in stories that make sense of it all. This "making sense of it all" is the art of bullshit. Our unique position as the species dubbed *"Homo Sapiens"* (translation from Latin: "Wise Man") gives us, in actuality, the responsibility to *create wisdom*. Once, we envisioned our responsibility as that of the discovery of wisdom, of truth, of fact. Now, I will argue in this essay, we have an even higher calling: we are the creators of truths from the raw material of observed facts. In sum, we are all called to be bullshit artists. And the universe, known and unknown, is the tapestry for our artwork.

Certain developments in science, in philosophy, and in popular literature support this thesis of the evolution of the human being to what I will now call *"Homo Bullshitter."*

Thomas Kuhn wrote of paradigm shifts: great changes in the framework for understanding reality that seem almost to change the nature of reality. For what is reality but that which we perceive it to be? What is reality but a shared vision, or dream? One example of a paradigm shift might be seeing the earth as the center of the universe first, and then seeing the sun as the center of a solar system around which the earth orbits. Then again, another shift would be a theory posited by physicist Stephen Hawking that each point in universe is actually the center of an ever-expanding universe. Which brings earth back the center, but surrounded by an infinite number of centers from which the universe expands in concert. These paradigm shifts, or great changes in ways of seeing phenomena, are like changes in pairs of glasses. Once changed, the phenomena we observe begin to fit the framework through which we view them. And throughout time and history there seems to be no end to number of glasses that we can try on for size. We are, as it were, in a glasses shop, picking and choosing among an infinite supply of lenses, looking for the "right" lenses, but not always appreciating how we are, in fact, the manufacturers and choosers of the particular lenses we wear at a particular point in time Mix in with this observation the current theory that you cannot observe a thing without changing the nature of that which is observed— that is to say, *observation is also creative.* How we choose to see a thing impacts what it is, as does how we describe the thing we observe. That's where bullshit comes in.

Let's not get too much into physics, though. It is a subject I know very little about. I am not a scientist. I may very well have screwed up the science, but nonetheless I have described the science *as I understand it.* As I understand anything, really. These ideas of *the science of bullshit* are merely incorporated into my identity, whatever that is.

In fact, in this *post-post-modern world*, I am very confused about what I am, for I am not a single thing. By vicissitudes of culture and of fate, I find that I must, in effect, *bullshit my identity* according to the context in which I find myself, and that context is ever changing. I do try to be authentic.

But what is authenticity?

At one point in my life, certain luminaries of the academic world taught me that *authenticity* itself was the corrupt construct of the worldview of *sentimental humanism*. They worked in the English department at the University of Pittsburgh. (If you ask me, Pittsburgh, though quaint, is an ideal city in which to stage the destruction of *sentimental humanism*. Very few people seem to want to live there, and those that do seem terminally stuck there and morbidly depressed. I personally enjoy the beer and the Primanti Brother's restaurant, where you can get a fried egg on a sandwich.)

Well, truth be told, *sentimental humanism* is really old hat. Maybe it was corrupt, who knows? We have many choices of cultural frameworks now. As of this writing, there are many other things in world other than *sentimental humanism* from which to select our preferred worldviews (that is, if we should decide to hand over the generation of a personal worldview to others rather than assume the task ourselves). There is, for example, *trans-humanism. Trans-humanists* believe that some lucky group of us will soon upload our consciousness into computers. Sound like bullshit? Who knows? As I hope you shall soon see, in a democratic society, we each have the right, if not the duty, to *invent our own bullshit*—and to be happy mucking about in it.

But what of good old *sentimental humanism*?

If you ask me, *sentimental humanism* is the narrative (or cultural story) that holds out as to be cherished values such as family, love, freedom of expression, human rights, even life itself. It is the worldview into which many of us are born. And to which many of us cling throughout life.

After birth, and a bit of growing up, some lucky few of us are introduced to the deconstruction of *sentimental humanism* that occurs in *post-modernism*. *Post-modernism* tears apart the values of *sentimental humanism* and shows them to be the ideals of an oppressive, predominantly white and Western culture, an ideology that protects myths of class and race, and which, though on its face innocuous, must be eliminated in favor of a worldview that is decidedly squishy but seems to be rightly controlled by a collection of progressive-style academic elites who believe their bullshit smells better than yours. Take this as you will—do not, however, be disheartened, if you are, as am I, a lover of intellectual freedom with a hint of sentimentality. There is hope yet. The hope lies in *you*.

III. The Cogito

"I think therefore I am, right?"
"No, not really. A fuller
formation of Descartes's
philosophy would be Dubito,
ergo cogito, ergo sum. 'I doubt,
therefore I think, therefore I
am.' Descartes wanted to know
if you could really know that
anything was real, but he
believed his ability to doubt
reality proved that, while it
might not be real, he was."
— **John Green (Turtles All the
Way Down**)

Perhaps you may have guessed that I was an English major and pursued graduate study in English literature at the University of Pittsburgh in the late 1990s, where I was first introduced to postmodern deconstruction. Perhaps you did not.

The question is: what does all this have to do with *bullshit*? I was supposed to give you a good definition of bullshit and I spent pages talking about theories of science and culture.

Let me tell you a little story then.

When I applied for a Master's at the University of Pittsburgh, my personal essay was quite flippant and I had no expectation of admission. (When they did admit me, with a fellowship, they made sure to express clearly that I was not their first choice.)

To make a long story short, my essay was about bullshit. I argued that all literary criticism was bullshit; however, I continued, bullshit, like manure, allows the flowers to grow. It is the very material from which flowers—or in this case the *meaning* of a text—is born. In short, we *need* bullshit, and bullshit is beautiful.

Some time into my course of study, I became immersed in the ideas of postmodernism. As a person raised Roman Catholic, I was particularly wedded to the idea of Truth with a capital "T" and postmodernism's central Truth is that there is no truth. Reality itself is fabrication, developed by consensus. Culture is a "narrative," a story we tell into which we squeeze ourselves. The empowering element of this idea is that we can release ourselves from a negative narrative (one that doesn't work for us) and re-write a positive one. The disempowering element is that if there is no Truth, then those with power can simply define reality for the rest of us, squeeze us into the narrative of that reality, and punish us in various ways if we do not fit. The latter idea was particularly irksome to me. I like the notion of being able to say, "We hold these Truths to be Self-Evident … etcetera." To be able to appeal to Universal Human Rights.

Well, there was a crusty old professor named Steve with whom I began to debate these matters. He would say such things as, "When I speak, it is not me speaking; it is the language of the Program of the Academy. I am just a vessel of the Program."

This made me think of Descartes. In one of his philosophical treatises, Descartes proposes that all of reality could be created by an evil demon and that reality could essentially possess us and speak through us. In such a reality, his very existence might be the illusion of the demon. But Descartes concludes that because he can doubt reality, because he can think about the reality of reality, therefore he exists: Cogito Ergo Sum ("I think therefore I am.")

To my mind, Steve hadn't quite gotten to that point. He was accepting that he was nothing but the creation of the evil demon—or in this case a programmatic course in English composition.

I sat down at his desk, and I asked him, "Is the theory of this Program prior to the Cogito?"

"Very few people would understand how to ask that question," he said.

"Well, I do, " I said. "What's the answer?"

Steve smiled. "It's prior to the Cogito."

Which is to say that Steve was, in his own mind, immersed in a reality that was an illusion, and that he and the other members of that English composition Program had not reached the conclusion, *I doubt, I think, therefore I am.*

Well, I doubted the whole Program, and I dropped out. But I learned some valuable lessons. There is great power in claiming the *right to think.* We need not let illusions created by others, be they demons or fellow human beings, govern the narratives (the stories) of our lives.

We can be *bullshit artists* ourselves.

B.S.

Appendix I: The Origins of Bullshit

At the time of this writing, there has not yet, based on m research into the matter, been published a thorough treatise on the origins of *bullshit*. The closest thing I found to a reputable treatise on bullshit was a philosophy book by one Harry G. Frankfurt called *On Bullshit.* It was a *New York Times* bestseller, so there must be great interest among the populace in nature of bullshit. Perhaps *my* booklet will also become a *New York Times* bestseller, though I fear that my *reverence* for bullshit may be off-putting to some readers with stuffy noses.

Nevertheless, an author like me, unknown to the world but full of wishful thinking, may always hope that his own *bullshit* will, by some miracle of fate, ascend to the number one position of the bestseller list of *any* newspaper, even the highly honored *New York Times.*

I must confess that I did not read Mr. Frankfurt's book about bullshit as it sounded somewhat tedious in the book description. However, as a practicing bullshit artist, I will write with some authority on his thesis based on the book description alone. This sort of thing is a hallmark of the bullshit artist, so here goes. In sum, Mr. Frankfurt lacks my own appreciation for the magic of bullshit, and its capacity to bring meaning to what could otherwise be a drab and humdrum existence. Certainly, he does not appreciate the rich aromas of bullshit, the many shapes, sizes, and formulations in which it may present itself in post-post-modern society. Instead, Mr. Frankfurt spends eighty odd pages distinguishing between the *bullshit artist* and the *liar*, and then claims that the bullshit artist is a greater enemy of truth than the liar because he (or she) has no appreciation of facts, whereas the liar *appreciates* the truth of facts but merely covers the facts up with deceit.

Now this thesis, though it may come from the pen of a professional philosopher, sounds just a bit like bullshit itself.

In fact, Mr. Frankfurt *may* just be philosopher who wanted to write a philosophical-sounding book about bullshit—perhaps because he thought it might propel him to the top of the *New York Times* bestseller list for its high-minded racy title—and then, when sitting down at table to write, proceeded to bullshit some intellectually styled sentences critiquing bullshitting, In fact, he went further than mere critique of bullshit. He vindicated *the liar* at the expense of the *bullshit artist*, failing to appreciate the contributions of the bullshit artist to the creation of meaning and beauty.

In fact, given the thesis of his book, one must wonder if Mr. Frankfurt himself is knowingly deceitful as an author and philosopher. Did he, in fact, write a book on bullshit, criticizing bullshit, knowing that what he was writing was going to be itself bullshit? In Mr. Frankfurt's mind, that deceit would be perhaps more palatable that pure bullshitting. You see, when executed properly, pure bullshitting does not concede the existence of underlying facts that conflict with the substance of the bullshit.

It's just bullshit.

In my mind, bullshit does not, however, threaten truth.

Bullshit *is* truth.

Now let's let Mr. Frankfurt alone and get into the true grit of the matter: what is the history of bullshit? Where did it originate? How did it evolve from its point of origin? (We'll save the answer to that latter question for Essay Two.)

First, bullshit has *always* existed, but our *awareness* of bullshit has not.

Few may have considered this, and even fewer scholars (masters themselves of bullshit) may agree with this thesis, but I believe that the philosopher Socrates initially exposed the *existence of bullshit* in the 5th century BC.

In the Socratic dialogues, as recorded by Plato, Socrates challenges the cultural assumptions of a number of purportedly wise individuals with whom he chats by asking a litany of discombobulating questions. The end result, typically, is that the individual's initial assumptions are abandoned and replaced by a confused sense of not knowing much about anything. Though the Oracle of Delphi is said to have stated that no man in Greece was wiser than Socrates, Socrates himself said he was wise only insomuch as was aware of his own ignorance, while other men were convinced of their own possession of certain facts. In sum, Socrates was a great "discombobulator," tearing through ancient Greece and exposing bullshit artists through logic games and questioning. And, ultimately, the bullshit artists in the Greek government put him to death.

Bullshit has a way of wanting to protect itself, one may suppose.

The interesting thing about Socrates is that he went to his death willingly. In some sense, he recognized the importance of the bullshit in which he was immersed, the cultural, philosophical, and religious suppositions in which he was spawned and which he spent his life challenging. So, in deference to bullshit, Socrates drank a cup of hemlock and perished.

Common sense among the general populace in our own times might be that bullshit is puffery that obscures facts— facts that may be uncovered through inquiry of some kind. But Socratic inquiry leads to a mental state in which facts are elusive, even unknowable.

In this way, Socrates lays the groundwork for *self-conscious* bullshitting as a process for stringing together observed phenomena into webs of meaning that become true by consensus. Whether he intended to or not, Socrates awakened humanity both to our own inherent ignorance and our capacity to fill the hole left by ignorance with *primo*

bullshit.

THUS ENDS ESSAY ONE ON *THE*

ANCIENT ART OF BULLSHIT. LOOK FOR

MORE ON THE HISTORY OF BULLSHIT IN

ESSAY TWO, COMING SOON TO AMAZON.

IN THE MEANTIME, GO FORTH AND

BULLSHIT WITH THE BEST OF THEM!

B.S.

Made in the USA
Lexington, KY
16 February 2019